Richard III

A Shakespeare Story

RETOLD BY ANDREW MATTHEWS
ILLUSTRATED BY TONY ROSS

ORCHARD BOOKS

For Rob
A.M.

ORCHARD BOOKS
338 Euston Road, London NW1 3BH

Orchard Books Australia
Hachette Children's Books
Level 17/207 Kent St, Sydney, NSW 2000
ISBN 1 84616 181 9 (hardback)
ISBN 1 84616 185 1 (paperback)
First published in Great Britain in 2006
First paperback publication in 2007
Text © Andrew Matthews 2006
Illustrations © Tony Ross 2006
The rights of Andrew Matthews and Tony Ross to be identified as the author
and illustrator of this work have been asserted by them in accordance with
Copyright, Designs and Patents Act, 1988.
A CIP catalogue record for this book is available from the British Library.
1 3 5 7 9 10 8 6 4 2 (hardback)
1 3 5 7 9 10 8 6 4 2 (paperback)

Contents

Cast List

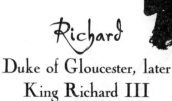

Richard
Duke of Gloucester, later
King Richard III

Duke of Buckingham
Follower of Richard

Henry Tudor
Earl of Richmond,
later King Henry VII

King Edward IV

Prince Edward
King Edward's son

Richard, Duke of York
King Edward's son

The Scene
England in the fifteenth century.

And therefore, since I cannot prove a lover
To entertain these fair well-spoken days
I am determined to prove a villain

Richard; I.i.

Richard III

Visit the battleground at Bosworth Field alone, and you will meet me without knowing it. My restless spirit will seem to be the sighing of the wind through the branches of a tree, or the creeping shadow of a passing cloud. Long ago, I was flesh and blood like you. I was a king until I came here. On this field I lost my crown, my kingdom and my life.

Before I became King Richard, I was Richard, Duke of Gloucester, son of the house of York, though my deformed back and withered arm earned me other titles. 'Richard Crookback', my enemies called me, 'hedgehog' and 'spider'. I had many names and many enemies, chiefly in the house of Lancaster.

For almost thirty years the Yorkists
and Lancastrians made war to decide
who would rule in England. My brother
Edward was king, until he was overthrown
and exiled by King Henry; but he came
back, with me and our brother George,
Duke of Clarence, at his side. King
Henry was imprisoned in the Tower of

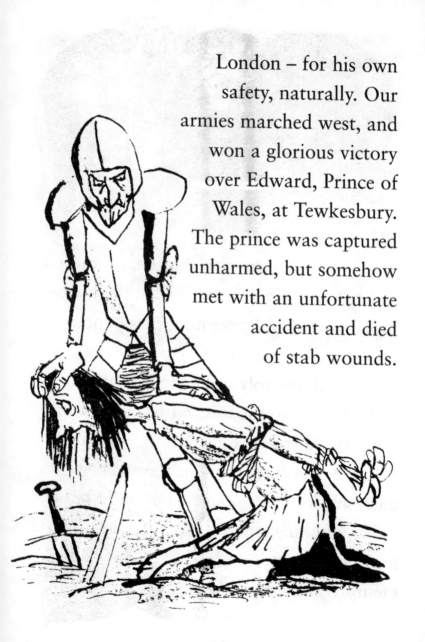

London – for his own safety, naturally. Our armies marched west, and won a glorious victory over Edward, Prince of Wales, at Tewkesbury. The prince was captured unharmed, but somehow met with an unfortunate accident and died of stab wounds.

While my brothers celebrated, I returned to London, paid a secret visit to the king in the Tower, and gave him the sad news of his son's death. Poor Henry was too gentle and too holy to live in this world, so I sent him to the next with the point of my dagger, and gave it out that he had died of grief.

The old king's tragic death set me thinking.

The Yorkists had triumphed over the Lancastrians, but the result was more like a truce than peace. Just below the uneasy surface lay mistrust, hatred and the desire for revenge. Given such a situation, it grieved me to consider what wickedness a mischievous person might do, simply by dropping hints and spreading rumours.

My way was clear. I could have supported my brother the king, and toiled to reconcile the houses of York and Lancaster, but peacemaking was not to my taste. The time was ripe for someone to play the villain, and I was determined to be that someone. I would deceive, and double-deal, and smile – even as I committed murder.

* * *

When wars end, the victors often fall out, and so it was with us; I made certain of it.

During his exile, my brother Edward was struck with a wasting disease that gave him a hollow cough, and stretched his skin tightly over his bones. With the throne regained, he ruled England, but his sickness ruled him. He feared plots against him, and spoke daily with astrologers, fortune-tellers and the like.

The night I received news that the king had issued a warrant for the arrest of the Duke of Clarence, I hurried to Clarence's house and met him in the street outside, accompanied by armed guards.

"Why has our brother Edward done this, Clarence?" I cried.

Clarence laughed carelessly.

"Because my name is George," he said. "Some half-crazed wizard told him that his sons would be cheated of the throne by a man whose name begins with G."

"This is the queen's doing!" I growled. "She encourages the king's wild imaginings." The captain of the guard saluted me.

"I'm sorry, my lord Gloucester, but I was given orders that no one should be allowed to talk to the prisoner," he said.

"Please stand aside, and let me do my duty."

"Very well," I agreed. "Don't worry, Clarence. I'll make sure that you're not imprisoned long."

16

As the guards marched their prisoner away to the Tower, I smiled to myself, for it was I who had taught the wizard what to say to the king, and paid him to say it.

"Ah, Clarence!" I sighed. "As your brother, I want only the best for you, and it would be best if your soul were safe in Heaven. I will arrange it soon, I promise you."

The first part of my plan had been successful. With a light heart, I made my way to Westminster to begin the second part – winning myself a bride.

* * *

The interior of the abbey was glowing
with candlelight. Great stone pillars
soared up into the darkness all around me
as I searched for the side chapel where the
coffin containing the body of the late
King Henry lay awaiting burial the
following morning. The coffin had been
placed on an altar, and draped with an

embroidered cloth. Before the altar,
dressed in mourning robes, Lady Anne,
the widow of Prince Edward. I had
heard her beauty praised, though she was
a little past her prime, but I had also
heard talk that she was weak-willed and
easily led. Now I was about to put the
rumour to the test.

Lady Anne turned as she heard me slip into the chapel. Her eyes widened in loathing.

"What black magician conjured you up, fiend?" she hissed.

I bowed. "I learned that you were keeping vigil here tonight, and I came to offer you my respects."

Lady Anne quivered.

"I don't want your respects, you filthy toad!" she raged. "I want the earth to open up and swallow you back down into Hell."

"I didn't know that angels could be so angry," I said, flinching. "Why do you speak so harshly to me?"

"You murdered my husband!" screeched Lady Anne. "So I did, but do you know why?" I retorted. "Because your lovely face burned in my every waking thought, and in all my dreams. The idea of you in someone else's arms was more than I could bear. Jealousy drove me out of my wits!"

Lady Anne's feelings showed in her look. She was both horrified and fascinated, as though she found me repellent, yet attractive.

Then came my master stroke.

I fell to my knees, drew my dagger, closed Lady Anne's hand around the hilt and bared my neck.

"If I can't have your love, give me your hate, and kill me!" I pleaded.

For a moment I thought that she would, but she faltered. The dagger dropped from her fingers and clattered on the flagstones.

I picked it up and pressed the edge of the blade to my throat.

"Tell me to kill myself!" I sobbed.

"No!" said Lady Anne. "No, I don't want you dead."

I gave her my most adoring gaze.

"But may I live in hope, my lady?" I murmured.

We were married five days later.

* * *

Though the king's health was failing fast, he ignored the doctors who advised him to rest, and insisted on holding a banquet to honour my new bride. Invitations were sent out to the great and good, and also to those who were not so good.

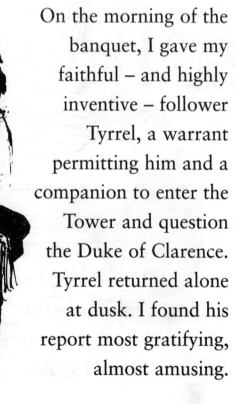

On the morning of the banquet, I gave my faithful – and highly inventive – follower Tyrrel, a warrant permitting him and a companion to enter the Tower and question the Duke of Clarence. Tyrrel returned alone at dusk. I found his report most gratifying, almost amusing.

At the banquet, King Edward proposed
a toast to the house of York, and added,
"I have good news concerning my brother
Clarence. I have signed his pardon, and he
will be set free tomorrow."

I waited for the murmurs of approval to
die down before I spoke.

"Your majesty," I said hesitantly. "Has no one informed you? Clarence is dead. He was found this afternoon in the cellars of the Tower, drowned in a barrel of wine. I often warned him of the dangers of drinking, but he paid me no attention."

The king fell back into his chair, and was wracked by a fit of coughing. Blood gushed from his mouth.

"Servants!" shouted Queen Elizabeth. "Carry the king to his bed. Call the royal physicians!"

As the guests waited for news of the stricken king, they broke into groups and chatted.

I found myself in company with the Duke of Buckingham, a man with a reputation for greed and treachery; I admired him.

"I wonder what the queen's brother, Lord Rivers, is discussing so earnestly with Lord Grey, Lord Hastings and the Earl of Richmond?" I said, as I poured more wine into Buckingham's goblet.

"How to thwart your ambitions, my lord," he replied.

I pursed my lips. "Oh, and do I have ambitions?"

"You desire to wear the crown, my lord," said Buckingham.

"Suppose I did wear it, would you be for me or against me?" I enquired.

Buckingham took a sip of wine.

"I am loyal to whoever can afford me," he said.

"Would the earldom of Hereford buy your support?" I mused.

Buckingham inclined his head. "My lord, I am your man."

At that moment, the doors of the banqueting hall flew back and Queen Elizabeth appeared. Her hair was in disarray, and tears lined her pale cheeks.

"The king is dead!" she announced. "His dying wish was for his brother, Richard of Gloucester, to be appointed Lord Protector, and given guardianship of our young sons."

It was neither the time nor the place for grinning, so Buckingham and I smiled at each other with our eyes.

* * *

And so I became guardian to my nephew Edward, Prince of Wales, who was twelve, and my namesake Richard, Duke of York, who was ten. Edward would be crowned king, and I would rule in his name until he was twenty-one.

This arrangement caused me some distress. To wield power for a few brief years, and then surrender it to my nephew seemed unsatisfactory to me. I thought long and hard about what obstacles lay between me and the throne, and how best to remove them. Buckingham and I burned out many candles in our secret night-time conferences, but our time was well spent.

The nation was rocked by a chain of sensational scandals. Papers came to light that proved Lord Rivers and Lord Grey were scheming to kidnap the young princes and hold them to ransom. The traitors were arrested, tried and beheaded.

To protect my nephews from other evildoers, I had them moved into the Tower, where I could keep a close eye on their welfare.

Meanwhile Henry Tudor, Earl of Richmond, suddenly left England for France.

Shortly after, my French spies reported that he was attempting to raise an army against me, but I was not alarmed by this. Henry Tudor had Welsh blood in his veins, and what Welshman had ever amounted to anything? More disturbing was a tale that Lord Hastings had boasted of how I would never be king while his head remained on his shoulders.

I had the strangest feeling that another shocking scandal was at hand.

It broke during a meeting that I called to decide on a date for my nephew's coronation. Hastings was present, along with Buckingham, Lord Stanley, and the Bishop of Ely.

Hastings made a long and flowery speech that ended with the suggestion that I should fix the day.

My response was a loud groan and a heavy sigh.

"Are you unwell, my lord?" asked Hastings.

"Sick at heart!" I replied. "Tell me, Lord Hastings, what sentence would you pass on those who used witchcraft to harm the royal family?"

"Why, death!" Hastings said without hesitation.

"Then you have passed sentence on yourself, my lord!" I exclaimed. "For you and the late King Henry's wife cursed me with your dark magic."

"No!" cried Hastings.

"No?" I echoed, raising my withered arm with its clawed hand for all to see. "If I was not cursed, how do you explain this?" Hastings's eyes were empty; I had him, and he knew it.

"I c–cannot explain it, my l–lord," he stammered.

The Bishop of Ely was dumbfounded.

"This man should stand trial at once!" he mumbled.

"No need for a trial," I said. "His guilt is written on his face. Guards, take Lord Hastings outside and put him to death!"

* * *

The hardest blow of all was quick to follow. Buckingham chanced upon an old chronicle that made it plain that my brother Edward, while still an infant, had been betrothed to the daughter of a French nobleman. The betrothal had long been forgotten, and its rediscovery had far-reaching consequences. It meant that Edward's marriage to Queen Elizabeth had been unlawful. My nephews were illegitimate, and so barred from inheriting their father's crown. Imagine my feelings when I heard of this!

Bands of Londoners took to the streets, calling for me to be made king. These loyal outbursts were arranged by Buckingham, who also led the delegation of city worthies who implored me to take the throne. I protested that I was weak and unworthy, but at last they persuaded me to put duty

before self, and I accepted the heavy burden of kingship.

Events moved swiftly. Two days before my coronation, I was told that Richmond had set sail from France, in command of an invasion fleet. I ordered my navy to sink it.

At my coronation feast, my wife Anne fell ill with stomach pains and sickness, and had to take to her bed.

That evening, Buckingham brought grave news to my private chamber.

"Gales have kept your navy in port, sire," he told me. "Richmond has landed on the coast of Wales. Lord Stanley and the Bishop of Ely have joined forces with him."

"Ha!" I scoffed. "After I've crushed them, I'll have their heads spiked on London Bridge." I lowered my voice. "Buckingham, issue a proclamation that the queen is fast approaching her death."

Buckingham raised his eyebrows. "Is she, sire?"

"If she is not, I paid good money to an apothecary who lied about the poison he supplied me with," I said. "The queen is too old to give me the male heir I need.

When I've put down this rebellion, I'll marry my niece Elizabeth. She's young and strong. Oh, and kill my nephews, would you?"

Buckingham cocked his head, as though he had misheard. "Sire?"

"My nephews are a threat to my royal
line. I want them dead!" I snapped.

"Majesty!" blustered Buckingham.
"Give me a little time to—"

"There is no time, Buckingham!"
I interrupted.

Buckingham stiffened. "I'm afraid
I must remind your majesty that you have
not yet kept your promise to make me
Earl of Hereford."

I smiled. "Promise, Buckingham?
I promised you nothing. Leave me. We
will speak again once your memory
has improved."

When Buckingham had gone, I softly
called out, "Tyrrel?"

Tyrrel flowed out of the shadows and
stood beside me.

"Sire?"

"I fear that Lord Buckingham will turn against me," I said. "He has no stomach for the business I discussed with him."

"Depend on me to deal with it for you, sire," said Tyrrel.

"Bear in mind that they are anointed princes," I warned. "Don't shed their precious blood."

"Not a drop, sire," Tyrrel vowed.

And he was true to his word, for later he described to me how he smothered my nephews.

* * *

War gathered like clouds in a stormy sky. More nobles deserted me for Richmond, including Buckingham, who was taken prisoner by one of my generals in the course of a minor skirmish. The general

sent me Buckingham's head, which
I regarded as a great kindness.

Richmond's forces marched east,
I marched my armies west to meet him,
until we faced each other at Bosworth Field.

The night before the battle, I dreamed that I was visited by the ghosts of my victims, who predicted my defeat.

I woke up in a cold sweat.

"My conscience gives me nightmares, but nothing else!" I muttered to the dark. "I won wealth and power without it, and made myself the man I am – the villain I set out to be!"

* * *

That sly viper Richmond outwitted me
and attacked before dawn, when my
forces were not fully prepared. His
artillery blew gaps in my front lines, and
his cavalry surged through. My soldiers
might have rallied, but my best

commander, the Duke of Norfolk,
was reported slain, and his troops
retreated in confusion. I tried to bring
up reinforcements, but the cowardly
Earl of Northumberland refused to obey
my orders.

The day was lost. The best that I could
hope for was to make my escape. Then
a volley of arrows cut my steed from
under me. I staggered through the smoke
of battle, shouting, "A horse! A horse!
My kingdom for a horse!"

As if in reply, a horse appeared: a dapple-grey war horse galloped towards me, with Henry, Earl of Richmond, on its back.

I saw him lean sideways, saw light flash on the blade of his battleaxe as he swung it...
My memories end there.

I was wrong about Henry Tudor – he amounted to something after all. My crown was placed on his head, and he founded a line of monarchs that lasts to this day, for his distant descendants still live in royal palaces.

As for me, I have shrunk to a breath of wind, a trick of the light. When I am remembered, if I am remembered, I am Richard the Bloody, Richard the Tyrant who slaughtered the princes in the Tower.

Well, it is better than being completely forgotten. In the end, villainy has granted me a kind of immortality.

God and your arms be praised, victorious friends!
The day is ours. The bloody dog is dead.

Richmond; V.v.

Villainy in Richard III

Richard III was Shakespeare's first great popular success, and it remains one of his most frequently performed plays.

King Richard is a villain so ruthless and cruel that he comes close to being a pantomime character. What saves him from seeming ridiculous is his dark sense of humour. His witty asides to the audience win us over to his point of view. More than simply a mindless thug, he deliberately sets out to manipulate the weak characters who surround him, and we share his relish when he succeeds.

Shakespeare wrote the play between 1592 and 1593. Though he based the plot on the best historical sources of the day, Thomas More's *History of King Richard the Third*, and Holinshed's

Chronicles, the real-life Richard Plantagenet was nothing like as evil as his stage counterpart. There is no evidence to connect him with the disappearance of the princes in the Tower, nor is there any conclusive evidence that they were murdered.

Henry Tudor, Earl of Richmond, who appears as a character in the play, became King Henry VII, father of King Henry VIII and grandfather of Queen Elizabeth I. Tudor historians were anxious to portray Henry Tudor as a noble hero who ended the reign of a murderous tyrant, and established peace and stability after a period of bloody civil war.

In no way should this lack of accuracy spoil our enjoyment of the play. Shakespeare was not a historian, but a dramatist whose genius is still able to transport audiences out of their everyday lives, and plunge them into the exaggerated life of the stage.

Shakespeare and the Globe Theatre

Some of Shakespeare's most famous plays were first performed at the Globe Theatre, which was built on the South Bank of the River Thames in 1599.

Going to the Globe was a different experience from going to the theatre today. The building was roughly circular in shape, but with flat sides: a little like a doughnut crossed with a fifty-pence piece. Because the Globe was an open-air theatre, plays were only put on during daylight hours in spring and summer. People paid a penny to stand in the central space and watch a play, and this part of the audience became known as 'the groundlings' because they stood on the ground. A place in the tiers of seating beneath the thatched roof, where there was a slightly better view and less chance of being rained on, cost extra.

The Elizabethans did not bath very often and the audiences at the Globe were smelly. Fine ladies and gentlemen in the more expensive seats sniffed perfume and bags of sweetly-scented herbs to cover the stink rising from the groundlings.

There were no actresses on the stage; all the female characters in Shakespeare's plays would have been acted by boys, wearing wigs and make-up. Audiences were not well-behaved. People clapped and cheered when their favourite actors came on stage; bad actors were jeered at and sometimes pelted with whatever came to hand.

Most Londoners worked hard to make a living and in their precious free time they liked to be entertained. Shakespeare understood the magic of the theatre so well that today, almost four hundred years after his death, his plays still cast a spell over the thousands of people that go to see them.

Orchard Classics
Shakespeare Stories

RETOLD BY ANDREW MATTHEWS
ILLUSTRATED BY TONY ROSS

Orchard Classics are available from all good bookshops, or can be ordered direct from the publisher: Orchard Books, PO BOX 29, Douglas IM99 1BQ.

Credit card orders please telephone 01624 836000

or fax 01624 837033 or visit our website: www.wattspub.co.uk

or e-mail: bookshop@enterprise.net for details.

To order please quote title, author and ISBN
and your full name and address.

Cheques and postal orders should be made payable to 'Bookpost plc.'

Postage and packing is FREE within the UK

(overseas customers should add £1.00 per book).

Prices and availability are subject to change.